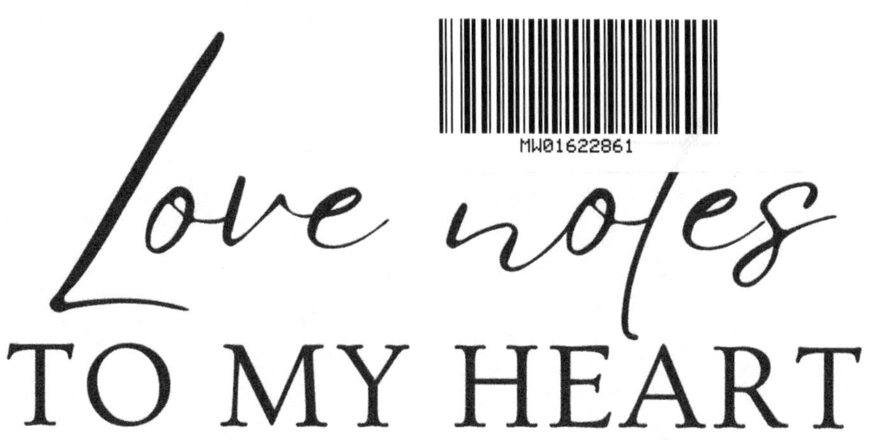

TO MY HEART

Writings about Wholeness,
Women, and the
Wild World

Jessica Ricchetti

Author of Wisdom of the Shadow and Wisdom of the Divine Feminine

Author: Jessica Ricchetti
Title: Love notes to my heart: writings about wholeness, women, and the wild world / Jessica Ricchetti
Design and cover image: Jessica Ricchetti
Edited by: Chelsey Moise, Deanna Jannuzzi, and Lumin Love-Star
Subjects: Spirituality, Self-Help, Nonfiction, Poetry.

This book was written and self-published on the unceded, systemically stolen Ancestral lands of the Tsalaguwetiyi (Cherokee, East), S'atsoyaha (Yuchi), and Miccosukee people. What is now commonly referred to as the Appalachian mountains in the region we know as Asheville, NC.

www.jessicaricchetti.com

ISBN: 978-1-7361794-4-4

I kneel at the altar of the most high.

The altar of my heart.

Of the beloved.

Of the all.

I ask that my heart be open, rooted, and pure

so that I may serve all

in the highest Devotion and Truth.

May it be so.

And so it is.

Dedication: To my beloved Jess,

You used to tell me I had a way with words, and how my writing was so impactful to your heart. You were the first person to tell me I was poetic in my expressions, nearly two decades before I believed that to be true in my own heart.

You knew me before I knew me. You were my first other half, who helped me feel whole, before I knew wholeness within myself.

When you left this world, a part of me left as well. It was the part of me that was the 'me', when we were we. The part of me that was a young girl, longing for so much. The part of me that ached, numbed, worked to fit in, and didn't yet KNOW herself.

If you were still walking this Earth alongside me, you'd say "see, I told you you should write". And yet, I hear you echoing this love in my heart. Always. In all ways.

I dedicate this book to you. Which also means I dedicate this book to me. The half of me that died, to remind me even more of my aliveness. The half of me that lives on in memory... Sometimes distant, sometimes close. The half of me that had so much hurt, pain, and secret traumas. The half of me that so innocently, and almost frivolously, loved and played. The half of me that nurtured me into knowing what it was like to be loved. The half of me that lives on sweetly now without holding the pains of the past. The half of me that dis-integrated to be so deeply integrated. The half of me that is eternal, holy, and absolutely whole. All of you. All of me.

I love you. Thank you for showing me myself.

XOXO - Jessica

Contents

Words

Nuance

Energy

Spelling

Dis-spelling

Weaving spells

Re-cognizing energy

Expressions of understanding

Mis-understanding

Miss. Understanding

Creating connection

Compassion

Communion

Creation

Calls

See

Key

Introduction

During a ceremony I was facilitating within a women's retreat, I felt a powerful flow of complete clarity, connection, and oneness within myself. I picked up my pen, opened my journal, and words flowed out... Divinely, potently, and so medicinally. I wrote a few 'poems' faster than I could think. *I use that word cautiously as someone who rebels against standard structures of writing that always felt more limiting than freeing to me when I was younger.*

In that moment, after writing a few pages, I wrote down "write a book"... and the title flowed afterwards, *"Love notes to my heart"*. I felt the potency of my ancestors with me, asking me to write this book. Not for them, for you reading this, or for any particular 'reader purpose'... Solely for my heart to express and share itself.

For months prior, I had been weaving words together in symbolic, mystical form as a salve to my heart, and as a way to make deeper, embodied sense of a wildly transformative time. Writing opened up a deeper magic within myself. I didn't truly realize this was happening until the Divine task of this book presented itself. This truly was a Divine task for me... I trusted in the mystery without needing to figure out what that was about. So, I devoted my YES to exploring my heart through writing these pages. I trust if you are reading this, there is medicine within these words for your heart.

This book became a collection of writings that poured out while being forged by the crucible of my soul's truth... a time where the deepest soul-ripping aches met the ecstatic brilliance of bliss... a time when writing was the only portal to my innermost sanctuary.

Why Love notes, Wholeness, Women, and the Wild World?

Love notes

Love is the language of the heart. I feel an infinite well of LOVE for life and all within it. I feel love for life's challenges, brilliance, and wholeness, love when looking at magical women, and love for the wild world that surrounds me. These writings are truly from my heart, to my heart. I trust that we are connected through one heart... and Love is its universal language.

Sometimes the most powerful medicine we have to offer others, are the wisdom nuggets we've collected as reminders to self. My wish is that these intimate pieces of my heart reach to the corners of your own, and that you may be soul-served by looking into the mirror of the heart of another.

Wholeness

Harmonious union and integration with all aspects of life.
A state of unbroken completeness.

I have worked hard for my Wholeness, as most people do... and I vow to myself to hold devotion to 'make whole' any parts of myself that feel un-whole, discarded, or divided from my heart. Writing about my experiences, challenges, griefs, aches, longings, feelings, and celebrations allows me to make beauty medicine from it all and more easefully integrate it into my holy wholeness.

Women

Sisterhood has brought a holy healing to my heart in ways I can likely only articulate a fraction of. Being in communion with women brought healing to the deep aches and longings for healthy relationship with women that began as a young girl. To witness the magic of women simply BE-ing themselves is immeasurably valuable to me. I write about women to celebrate, honor, witness, reflect, and uplift them/me/us.

This is not with a heart of exclusion, rather a heart of reclamation. I hold women with an inclusive definition that can be interpreted by your own heart. Any she/her/women language I use is because these words are the art I choose to reach my own soul's healing-places. They are simply reflections of myself and my life. Women are f*cking magic, and I am here for it!

The Wild World

The Earth and her trees, plants, flowers, mountains, rivers, streams, animal kin, stones, mycelium, fires, elements, and all beings who vibrate on this planet alongside us... are who I think of as the wild world. The world lives on around us wild and whole, with primal, innate, imprinted living intelligence. Reclamation of this wild within each of us, and living with a liberated spirit, is close to my heart - a re-learning of the simple intelligence of the world and its cycles within. Also, the 'world' we live in is a wild one... so some of my writings are about that as well.

I AM ONE

WITH AND AS

ALL THAT IS

SACRED

Wholeness

How delicious the nectar

Of the sweetest remembering

After a long dark night

Of holy forgetting

Divine Altar

Being in a relationship
with the Divine
doesn't take pain away.

It makes an altar
of beauty and prayer
for pain itself
to have a sacred space
so it may unfurl
its truth and tendrils
and have a place
to belong
exactly as it is.

Wound and wisdom
meeting one another
for a medicinal alchemy
honoring both/and.

When you sit with me

When you sit with me,
sit with all of me.
Exactly as I am.

Please don't linger
on the words of my sadness
and let them stir your own.

Please don't try to extend
moments of joy
to ease your own heart.

Simply sit with me,
in the wholeness
of all that I am, as I am.

Hold me as I am holding me.
See my grief as medicine,
so I can drink it up like an elixir.

See my power underneath it all.
For a moment of emotion,
doesn't change the shape of who I am.

Sit with me.
Just sit.
With me.

Reach in

We encourage reaching out
and not suffering in silence

What about reaching in
to the inner sanctum of stillness

What if we honor
the emptiness
as Sacred

Rather than
something needing
to be filled

These lows
these holy holes
are wholeness places
to find truth
and know ourselves
more deeply

Don't suffer in silence
reach in to the stillness...

Being Birthed

All I've ever known is tightening all around me,
constricting my movement and very being.

Faint sounds echo, beckoning me into "what is to come",
yet I cannot make out voices or words.

The womb of the holy dark pushes against me,
I've outgrown my stay... but I'm holding on tight.

I'm terrified of what is to come. I don't know where I'll go,
who I'll become, or who will be there to meet and support me.

I'm suddenly wailing. Through squeezed-closed eyes,
there is a light so bright I can't see.

I'm in another world now, cold and flailing,
wishing to be back in the warm, nourishing, comfort of the womb.

Suddenly, I am wrapped in the arms of the Divine mother,
and I breathe in a new sense of home...

Let yourself crumble

Let yourself crumble

Fall open

Receive
Share
Release
Rewrite

Don't wait to crack open
Don't hold back the truth

Just share
Just be as you are
Just express it as it is

Awaiting the perfect moment
doesn't make it come

The only moment
is right now

And it is as Divinely perfect
as any moment can be

Breaking Open

This is a breaking open
A full release in motion

Not from my trying
But through story-less crying

I release, I let go
I open my heart to greater flow

And then I sink in
Deeper than bone and skin

The Deep Ache

Deep blue-green waters circle around
Encapsulating with a sacred darkening
So fully that nothing can be seen clearly

Thrashing around through rip currents
Treading wild tides barely able to catch breath
No boat or shore or relief in sight

Exhausted from the struggle of staying afloat
Wishing to be consumed by the sea
For the thought of a single moment of respite

A split second in time before such surrender
Deep waves calm and flow with steady ease
Steady ground rises up from the salty abyss

Mother whale breaches the surface
Singing her songs of ancient remembering
Echoing healing codes back into my bones

A short visit

Melancholia has fallen upon me again
but I no longer become her.
We simply cuddle up together
for a short visit.

Sharing stories, songs, and tears.
Reminding one another
who we are,
then releasing each another
to walk our own ways.

The Infinite Well

The ache is so great
like an infinite well

Heart breaking open
a gaping hole of longing

A single drop in the well
ripples through each cell

Vibrating alive the waters
that have stayed still since the last disturbance

This infinite well holds
ALL the griefs, pains, and hurts

Felt so deeply
as if each one comes alive again

And it does
these living waters remember

They hold each tear
that has ever been cried

But drawing water
from this same well

Is exactly what creates space for the
most beautiful deep feelings of bliss

Never one without the other
both holy and whole

Perhaps if the tears stop
dripping into the well

One by one
waking the ancient pains

The well's waters
will remember stillness

And bliss can be consumed
without the ache

But each drop in the well
ripples through each cell

And the ache and longing
are stirred up yet again

The old ways of relating no longer serve.

The old ways of relating no longer fit.

The old ways of relating no longer work.

The old ways of relating no longer align.

The old ways of relating no longer connect.

I release them

from needing to show up and protect.

I lean in to deepened,

matured relating...

to *serve connection*

in more soul-aligned ways.

Salted bath , Salted tears

I was afraid my tears
would meet the saltwater
of my bath
and consume me
as they poured
into one another

Welling up
from the infinite well

Knowing the stories
of one another's origins
as stormy seas
I feared their
desire to merge
back into one

Instead
the living water
embraced me
and held sacred
the anointment
of my truth
wrapping me
in it's comfort
until each tear
was set free
gently trickling down
copper pipes
back into the Earth below

You have sat
at the altar
of pain
so many times
it knows you by name
and breath.

There is nothing left
to fear.

At all.

You can hold all
that comes your way...
while holding beauty
in the other hand.

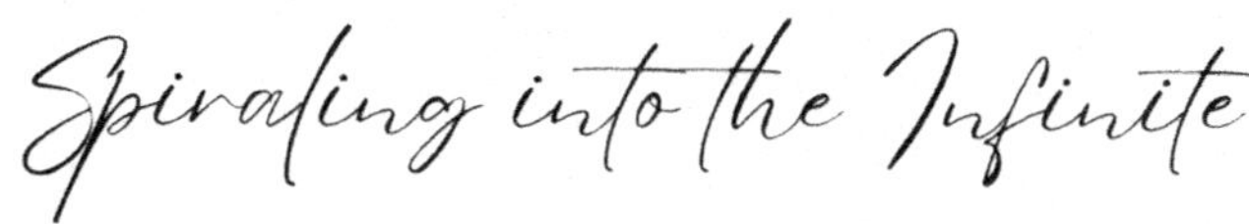

You are not infinitely spiraling, though it may seem exactly that.

You are spiraling into the infinite, there is a difference...

Trust that you'll reach a point where you've dissolved completely.

Letting go of all you thought was necessary and "you".

It may take longer and feel larger than you wish it to.

Your wishes are arbitrary, the mystery holds something greater.

Here, the cosmos take over, breaking you from attachments.

Returning you to your simplest form, one with stardust in the void.

There, you'll reach the center of the center,
and you'll know your spiral is returning you to you.

It will take time from there, for that is not the end, but the center.

The journey you took to get there will be mirrored on the way out.

Like a mirror, what you see is inverted. Same sight, different eyes.

So travel well and Trust the holy dark, it knows where it is going,
as only it knows where you've been.

And only from here, do you becoming anew.

Shadows call
And shadows fall

But shadows aren't really
Fearful after all

I woke up to rain

I woke up to rain
trickling down, then outpouring effortlessly
pooling faster than it could dissipate

forecasts didn't predict it
clouds must've gotten too full
the heaviness became too much to hold

it wasn't sky-rain, it was eye-rain
falling from cumulate-grief
emotion-storms and overcast minds

all I could do was watch it
embracing waters of sadness with open arms
unable to keep myself dry

I sat in it til I was bone-soaked
eventually it slowed, then stopped
and I was left with a rinsed-clean heart

Psychedelic Sadness

lean into your potent tears
until they carry you
through crystalline portals

through sacred geometry
of salted holy waters
pouring out like ocean tides

enter the growing pathway
meeting your eyes like a bridge
so you can see with crystal clarity

trace each tear back
to the sacred thread
from which it was birthed

sit with that single thread
until it tells you
it's greatest longing

hold that longing
noticing and feeling
breathing in the wisdom

until it changes
shape, form, and color
to in-form the path forward

cover your closed lids
with loose palms and tenderness
in prayer and reverence

create a container
to hold your tears where they are
amplify the visions in fertile darkness

listen so deeply to solely the hum of your heart
until the imprint of tear's sound
can be as seen as it is felt

travel into and through
the places of grief
not around them

until they tell you
who they are
by name and face

be altered
literally moved to the
altar of the heart

lean in
all the way in
even deeper in

until all the way in
becomes
through

it is time to surrender
into holy hope
and trust

for a pathway
- not yet seen -
to emerge

unfolding itself
precisely
in the moment of need

Let it be so
Let it be so
And so it is

Chaos

Into the wild waters
Chaos running free
Into the wild waters
I am the daughter of the deep

I will rise and
I will float
I will ebb and
I will flow

Into the wild waters
Chaos running free
Into the wild waters
I am the daughter of the deep

I'm deep in the cauldron...
One I know intimately,
a close familiar...

Fire underneath me,
scorching my stuck parts,
bubbling over and out...

Call to Prayer

This is a call to prayer...
Prayers. Blessings. Spells. Words of Remembering.
Big prayers.
Prayers as YOU weave them.
Hold the flame prayers...
Sit at the actual altar prayers...
Spoken aloud prayers.
Prayers that stir you until you feel stirred enough
to send them out...
Prayers that wake your ancestors...
Prayers that don't care how they are called by name...
Prayers that rattle your bones.
Ritual prayers.
Ceremonial prayers.
Actionable prayers.
Shake you awake prayers.
Forget who you are prayers.
Remember who you BE prayers.
Prayers that reach the depths of the inner cauldron...
The bottom scorched bits...
The seasoned bits.
Then
Sink into the formless...
And allow yourself to receive those prayers...
For your highest good.

You've walked
through the fire

Your warrior heart
has been forged
by crucible flames

Allow your tired feet
a moment of rest

Enough is enough
it is time for ease

Surrender

I surrender
into the portal
of the unknown.

Just when I think I "know"
or have the clarity I desire,
I lean into it,
and it shifts form
into something else
entirely.

I'm learning
a deepening
of non-attachment
to anything
at all...
not a being, place, or feeling.

When I'm pendulating,
oscillating,
dancing the sacred dance,
drinking in the fluidity
of water and wind,
remembering to breathe...

I surrender it all again.

Oscillating

Oscillating.
Ebbing and Flowing.
In the actual depths.
Not the gentle release and slow flow of a low tide,
but the thrashing into darkened waters, barely treading,
and ecstatic splashing of bliss crashing into itself.

This is the test.
The challenge.
The put your money where your mouth is.
The 'can I walk my talk?'
The opportunity for energetic attunement.
The consistent Soul-requirement of Devotion.

Contracting. Expanding.
Moment to moment.
Yes. No.
Both. And. All.
Everything. Nothing.

This is deep prayer time.
Dive into self time.
Time for ritual in action.
Time to extend instead of stretch.

Breathe.
Again.
Breathe.
Again.

Dance freely...
To RE-member.
Forget.
Remember.
All so quickly the linear can't keep track,
as it need not to.

Letting myself be worked.
So the work can work.
No stone unturned.

Fuck the old rusty plow.
And iron weights holding it down.
I release you.
I allow the old ways of relating to see themselves out.
I say YES to breathing and walking forward,
without efforting against the grain.
Simply. Joyously. Remembering-ly.

Breathe.
Remember.
Forget.
Breathe.

Drink the nectar.
Zip away.
Return.
Sip the succulence.
Fly free.
Return again.
Breathe.

I've rebirthed myself 1,000 times.

Each time with a different form.

Shapeshiting into the infinite...

And always coming right back

into this Sacred body.

Unraveling

My very own hands
created a mis-woven tapestry
filled with knots and misalignments
caught up from a mindless flow
not realized until years in the making

Painstakingly, I unravel this beloved cloth
teasing apart the threads
that weren't quite right
every loop and knot
stitch by stitch, one by one

What remained was a single thread
perfectly intact, beautifully aged
shapeshifted by fingers fiddling in prayer
almost as if completely anew
though familiar like a dear friend

Untangled yarn now spooled up neatly
wisened in its own rite and remembering
ready and calling to be created again
with boundless potential
for anything it wishes to become

Dearest Beloved,

Just BE.

Don't seek, long,
ask, or wish.

Just BE.

This is my prayer for you.

Her Crossroads

Standing at the crossroads.
One path with a clear vision of what's to come.
Another with a dream seed of new beginnings.
The third a complete mystery.

Hekate holds her lantern to illuminate the steps forward.
An offering must be made to her.
Not a small one... but one of the greatest value.
Something wildly loved that doesn't want to be let go of.
It's the only way. She won't receive any less.

I have sat at these very crossroads for years.
Clinging to the one thing I must let go.
It is time now. I feel it beckoning from the marrow of my bones.
So I lay it all down. She waits until it is all laid out. All, all, all.
I give up comfort and great love.
To step directly into the mystery.
Into what feels like fear and uncertainty.
And I walk it in Trust.

With first steps taken...
The clamoring noise of familiar fears fade away.
Each step more serene than the last.
A new comfort is unfolding.
What the path ahead holds doesn't need to be known.
I simply need to trust my feet, and know she knows the way...

It is Time Now

You feel the call of the wild
and notice where you have been
living in the tamed package
you boxed yourself into
for safety and comfort.

But you feel it...
The call for more.
The call to expand.
The need to spread your wings.
The ache to stretch open into bigness.

Your body tells you.
Your heart tells you.
Your soul tells you.
The trees and wind tell you.

But then the mind swirls,
with it's convincing stories.
And for some reason,
its singular voice
overtakes the community
of sacred ones calling you.
I forgive you,
the mind is simply doing its work
of analyzing and assessing.

And. It is time now.

Forgive the hyper-analysis
and trepidation.
Allow it to go on in the background.
Do not wait for it
to get on the same page.
Because it may not ever do so.

It is time now.
To let your body lead.
To be guided by your soul.
To be led by your heart.
To take your mind by the hand
and show it that it can come along
exactly as it is.

Because it is time now.
To step forward
into the unknown,
into the stretch of the new,
into the mystery,
and into that which is calling you.

Listen.
It is time now.
Walk forward.
It is time now.
Trust.
It is time now.

Saying no
to something
you love
and desire
more than anything,

because there is
a different yes
pulling the soul,

is a most difficult
and necessary step
towards freedom.

Release

I release what needs to be released.

Without needing to do anything else,
prove to have worked through it enough,
or have unwavering belief in my worthiness.

I don't need to convince myself with more ritual.

It can simply be complete and be released as it is.

There's nothing more to do but simply release.

And so I release.
And so it is.

Let the voice of the heart

be heard more clearly than

the voice of the mind.

Let the voice of the soul

be heard more clearly than

the voice of the heart.

Getting it all wrong

I was so worried about getting it all wrong.
Making the wrong decisions,
missing out on the signs directing me towards my purpose,
going against Divine order,
and living below my potential...

That I was missing out on the signs
telling me ALL is in Divine order.
And so I was, in turn, living below my potential,
because I was drowning myself in so much worry
and wrong-making that it consumed me.

So I decided to live without a line
defining if I was above or below anything.
And I remembered, with Trust, that there is no way
to go against Divine order, or get it wrong
when my purpose is simply to BE.

I don't need to think forward.

I don't need to think back.

I only need to tend to this moment

and walk it step by step.

Dearest Woman

You have been crying and aching long enough. Long. Enough. So much that you've summoned the seas through your eyes, and filled ancient wells.

That's enough. More than enough. You've shed plenty of tears as an offering to the altar of your healing. No more!

It's time to shift the wailing into howling. Use your voice now to yell prayers of ENOUGH and NO MORE. When you feel the old wells, welling up behind your eyes... Gaze into them and scry, not cry... Vision into new potential.

Look through the veils and see flames of blessings and healing held for your remembering, held by the ones you've tended - who have also been tending you. Let THEIR voice move through you until yours becomes one with the fire again.

Love,

Yourself.

Ironic, how taking
the exact step
that feels most
fearful

through the doorway
of the great
unknown

illuminates the very
path
that was just
shrouded
in a veil of mystery

Lean all the way in

Great magic happens
when we lean all the way in
to what our souls are longing for

when we gather enough courage
to press against the membrane of our fear
and say "I'm moving forward anyway"

suddenly, the illusion of suffering
we made bigger than it needed to be
fades away into the mystery

and everything we trusted
shows up to support
exactly what we needed all along.

All I think
All I know
All I think I know

is here

now

already so.

It is

already so.

And so I know...

All I think
All I know
All I think I know

is here. now.

It is already so.

Learning to weave

we can't learn
to weave

without first
picking up
the thread

and trusting
we will learn
along the way

the thread knows
its purpose
is to be woven

it holds the
remembering
and will teach

through Divine flow
of our fingers beckoning
the desire to learn

Each prayer is a remembering
of what is already so.

All you desire in prayer,
simply ask.

Don't ask to receive.
Don't wait to know.

Simply ask.

Ask to remember
that it is already so.

And so it is.

Love beyond measure

I sit
in the holy dark

lit by a single flame
dancing upon the ceiling
and the backs of my eyes

air fragranced
by fully blossomed roses

and the simple reminder
that I am loved

beyond measure

because I am love
beyond measure

This morning's prayers
were wild-danced
and soul-sung
to the forest...

skin to wind,
me to leaves...

the Earth's rumble
under my feet
shaking me
back into my bones...

Heart's Plea

Please, Practice Putting your feet on the Earth

Release Routine and Ruts with every breath

Always Align and Attune to the Sacred

Yes your You-niqueness and Yin-like flow

Ever Eager for Expanding the heart's mind

Right Relationship and Reverence blossoms abound

I Remember.

I am the Medicine.

Not in theory.

In walking Devotion
to every moment
as Sacred
exactly as it is right now.

I Return

I return to myself
with crystal clarity
in an elevated plane of awareness
with the consciousness of ease vibrating my cells
and my root ball rewiring me.

I am the love I desire.
I am everything I seek.

You are not powerless.

Stand up and speak clearly.

Use your voice without wavering.

Take your power into your own hands.

I Vow to My Truth

I will not let words
fall out
of my mouth

landing
on the ground
unmet

collecting dust
becoming litter.

My voice
shall be spoken
with intention
and devotion

into outstretched ears
who are equipped
to receive them.

I vow to watch
as my truth
is crafted well
and heard well.

Lean into that which brings you beauty

Lean out of that which brings you pain

The Alchemy of Ease

I have traveled the astral realms
Tasted the medicine of ceremony
Experienced the alchemy of expansion
Danced the waves of freedom
Breathed through the eternal
Witnessed myself in visions through time
Charted the constellations of my being
Written and held the sacred rituals

And now, all I crave
Is the simplicity of being
Exactly as I am
Exactly where I am
Exactly how I am
In Divine Perfection
Exactly as it is
And so it is

Well-spent moments

Not every moment needs to be 'well spent'.

We don't need to be endlessly
'tuned in'
'conscious'
or mindfully working on ourselves.

We don't need to prove our enoughness
to ourselves or anyone
by creating, 'doing', or meditating.
We don't need to consistently analyze our traumas or choices.

It's more than okay to just be.
In fact, it is vital.
It's okay to play.
It's okay to be human.
It's okay to read something that isn't 'spiritual'.
It's okay to choose mindlessness at times without needing to
navigate 'why', or without being 'guilty by disassociation'.
It's okay to release the shame
that comes with internal pressures of 'spiritual enoughness'.
It's okay to not always be navigating our assessments.

It's okay to just be.
It's more than okay to just be.
In fact, it is vital.

Holy. Mundane. Home

Leaky sinks and
Finicky faucets

Make things dirty
And then wash them

Round and round
The mundane we go

Forgetting all along
This is the holiest place

Home

Trust

TRUST
in the path of Ease
laid out before you...
by those who have walked before
and by YOU
who has walked before.

TRUST
in the deepening
that already is.
Trust in the deepening
beyond the limitations
of what
has already been.

Align

Align your heart with your heart's desire.

Align your soul with your passionate fire.

Align your body with it's sacred bliss.

Align your mind to remember this.

Deep Groove

I know now the imprint of what I'm yessing.
The new pathway has shown itself
and I breathe an exhale of relief.
I let this ease find it's way into and through
every cell of my being
so I may know it and learn it intimately.

I trust it will take time
for this new pattern
to become a deep groove...
Creating itself over time.

While this pathway is becoming itself
I might automatically trek
down the old one I know so intimately,
forgetting, temporarily, there is a new way.
Until the deep groove of the new way
becomes the well trodden path
my heart knows and trusts so fully.

Pathways don't become pathways overnight.
But I trust this single step
is a step
that will carve itself
through mud and fallen leaves
to guide my way on...

Roadmap to an Open Heart

There is a path to an open heart
with joy, bliss, and ecstatic expression...
And a roadmap to guide us exactly there.

If they explained the map before we were invested,
we may reconsider...
But we are already here now.

It begins by entering
the greatest crevice in the heart
and going deep, deep, deeper in...

Sifting through silt and muck,
the muddied corridors and collected dust.
We meet the depths of ache which give contrast as a prize...

At times we may wish we didn't enter the gaping heart opening,
since we can no longer turn a blind eye to the ache.

Though after a while,
we learn that our ability to hold our most brilliant light
is forged by our willingness to explore our darkest shadow.

The roadmap only guides us where to go,
we must be willing to go there
and embrace the journey along the way.

Accept me

As I am

Or leave me

As I am not

The Same Me

I see with my same eyes.
I dream with my same heart.
Almost as if nothing has changed at all.
Yet it feels like an entirely different ME.

So much has changed.
As if nothing remains.
All of myself has fallen away.
So more of myself can reclaim her space.

Each cell feels like it has
birthed itself into a new life.
And yet the lingers of my system
Always remember who I have always been.

To my most Ancient Self

Oh Holy Ancient One,

I wish to Remember

T H I S
Thisness

This very Thisness
RIGHT HERE
and
NOW

This simplicity of LOVE,
BEINGNESS, oneness,
and the Mystery beyond...

I wish to remember
the self
underneath
my self.

The self underneath the fear.
Not a self without fear...
I know that not to be true.

I wish to remember
the self underneath.
With the fear still present at the surface,
but the I AM
that is the
infinite deep.

Ancient self,
know my heart.

The heart I don't know
for it is buried
underneath
the known.
The NO.
The NO-thing.
The everything.

I am the knowing.
The unknown.
The never to be figured out.
The no.
The no-thing.
The every thing.

From my most Ancient Self

Dearest One,

You Remember.
You Know.
You BE.
You See.

You Forget.
You fret.
You BE.
You See.

BUT

You Remember.
You Know.
You BE.
You See.

Love,
~ YOUr most Ancient Self

When the mind speeds up
and is no longer
at the pace of the heart...
Slow down
Slower

When lack of knowing
and longing for clarity
begin spiraling and swirling...
Slow down
Slower

When equilibrium gets shifted
and center doesn't feel close...
Slow down
Slower
Slow...

I am worthy.
I am enough.
I am valuable.
I am needed.
I am wise.
I am true.
I am love.
I am you.

Thrive Era

This is my Thrive Era
My Alive Era
My licking honey from the hive Era

This is my Queen Era
My BE Era
My focusing energy on ME Era

This is my Vitality Era
My Beauty Era
My knowing I am perfect as I am Era

This my Abundance Era
My Rich Era
My overflowing with good Love Era

This is my Trust Era
My Alignment Era
My everything shed but Truth Era

This is my Pleasure Era
My Heaven Era
My 'I am a Sacred Treasure' Era

This is my YES Era
My Sexy Era
My receiving everything I desire Era

This is my Thrive Era

Women

Women Thrive.

Blossom and Become

To the woman I am becoming...

Your time has come to blossom.

I planted the seeds under the new moon.
Watered the soil with tears and rain drops.
Offered ripe, freshly nutrified compost.
Waited patiently for your cycles of dormancy.
Placed you lovingly in balance of sun and shade.
Sung songs and spoke poetic prayers.

And now...

It is time.

I see you budding and growing strong...
The Earth is warming just for your opening.

Open, open, open...

Let it be known

Let it be known!

I remember who the fuck I am.

I am Priestess.
I am Goddess.
I am Woman.
I am Queen.
I am ME... ALL of ME.

I walk my life for ME.
I reclaim ME.
I am falling in love with ME.
I am Devoted to ME.
I am here for ME.

And so it is.
And so it always was.

And so I am eternally grateful for the medicine
and lessons my soul has chosen for me...

I see now.
I BE now.
I AM now.

Oh, Dearest Woman...

I hope you Know,

Really Know,

The Full Potency

Of Your ALLness.

Women are Magic

Manifestations musing from our minds
Spells sprouting like seeds from our souls
Prayers presencing themselves playfully
Bliss beautifully blossoming from our bodies
Heaven healing us from here in our hearts

All we have to do is

Say it
Feel it
Know it
Believe it
Remember it
Think it
Trust it
See it
Be it

And we become it

Most Beautiful Sight

One of the most beautiful sights
I've ever seen
is a Woman
Reclaiming herself
Remembering her power
Realigning her life
Reawakening the sacred
Recognizing her brilliance
Relearning her beauty
and
Recreating her world

Her Body

Her body is of the mountains

Sharply carved by easterly winds

Curves softened by the living waters

Peaks reaching into blue-skyed heavens

Valleys meeting darkened depths

One with Earthen soil

Ancient stones as bones

Pathways lead to the undiscovered

Life blossoms external

Gaze deepened into caverns internal

Hollow bowl holding the infinite

Secrets under cover of stone

Expansive beyond what can be seen

Small as a pebble when far away

Strong enough to move the land itself

Still enough to simply BE

To me

Sweet Woman

Powerful Woman

Dear Woman

Deer Woman

Forgetful Woman

Full of regret Woman

Let it go Woman

Set it down Woman

Unleash Woman

Remember Woman

Together Woman

Inside it all Woman

Hear the call Woman

Love it all Woman

Hug yourself Woman

It's never done Woman

She will love you Woman

There is nothing wrong Woman

Just be love Woman

and it is done Woman

Conspiring Women

There are hidden pockets
Of women

Who are conspiring
And co-inspiring

Ways to secretly
Spread more magic

All over the world
And so it shall be done

His Gaze

I felt his penetrating gaze
wanting to keep me small
looking at me with discomfort
as he saw me in my fullness

I watched the shame
pour out from his body
in the direction of mine
and I drank it up as my own

Slowly, I sipped the poison
of becoming good enough
for him, for them
until I fell ill with disseverance

My own medicine
bitter and blame-spiked
curdled with disillusionment
disguised as love

With eyes wide open
I swallowed the sweet antidote
of choosing myself
dismantling the self-restriction

The ache of contortion
slowly dissolved
leaving nothing behind
but all of me

My Gaze

May I re-center my gaze,
living solely for my own approval.

May I catch the gaze of my own heart,
and let myself be taken away by the beauty.

May I look upon my life and see
what I wish to be seeing.

May the only gaze I am curious about
be my own.

Slowwwww down.

Invite in Ease.

Rest. Truly rest.

Without apology or shame, rest.

Restore.

Repeat.

Breathe

Breathe, woman.

Let your belly fluff out.
Inhale deeply.
Soften your jaw.
Relax your shoulders.

So many ways, they have told you to be.
Let your breath be for you.
Don't hold it back.
Let it flow.

Remember yourself as it ebbs and flows.

Breathe again.

And again.

And again.

She Remembered

She REmembered that she is the ALL...
Maiden, Mother, Queen, Crone, betwixt & between.

She REmembered to BE...
To BE all. To BE nothing. To just BE. Like the Bee.

She REmembered that SHE is worthy of honoring...
To be celebrated, cared for, cherished.

She REmembered herself as ALL of the elements...
Born of the Earth, Wild and Free.

She REmembered the old ways...
Where Rites of Passage were ceremonially honored.

She REmembered how to be loved...
How to receive care, connection, compassion, touch.

She REmembered how to move...
Unbound, untamed, fully seen... Fully. Seen.

She REmembered how to honor death...
Of the old illusory bones and the stories they held.

She REmembered a new way...
Of being birthed into a village who welcomed her.

She REmembered herself as The Dragon...
Wisdom, Power, Love, Ferocity, Gentleness.

She REmembered an imprint of actual magic...
That weaves itself into form beyond imagining.

She REmembered Nectar, Nourishment, Love...
In her body, as her body, in the body of her sisters.

She REmembered the songs that sing themselves...
That rise up from the Mystery & Presence.

She REmembered Sacred Union Within...
A true holy marriage of Wholeness and Love.

She REmembered to let it all go, to rest, to receive...
And that if you don't, you will.

She REmembered where the Nectar is found...
Right here, right now, as everything already is.

She REmembered...

She REmembered...

She REmembered...

To the Woman who has let herself go

Wow, Sister.
You have really
let yourself go.

Turn around.
Let me look at you.
I don't know what to say.

Your wildness
is taking away my breath.

I can see it. You've let yourself go.

You've really let yourself go...
deep into the forest, into the unknown.
Reclaiming your wildness,
with the Earth on your skin.

You've let yourself go.
To the hidden corners in your soul,
to disentangle yourself from
the webs of lies they tried to weave
around your heart
telling you what beauty should be.

You've let yourself go.
To the place within you
that let you burst from the boxes they placed you in...
And you carved a new path.

Damn sister. You've really let yourself go.

I see the wildness in your hair.
Stories of Elders and Ancestors
woven as silvery threads of magic
and mystery
pouring forth
from your head.

I see your bare skin.
Raw like freedom and truth.
Unabashed and unafraid.

I see the wisdom creeping in to your skin.
With little lines.
Like a road map you created
to find your way home.

I see the laughter
on your cheeks and eyes...
It has marked you,
forever unable to forget
that you have loved and lived.

I see your heart.
Shining brighter than jewels.
Adorning your glow
with sprinkles and sparkles
of glimmering hope.

You have really let yourself go.

I see your body.
How it whispers curvaceous love
and sensual stories.
How it has moved...
So strong and free.
How it howls with a life well lived.

I feel the Earth quake as you walk by.
As she wriggles and whirls
to celebrate each step you take.

I see your hands.
How they have worked
the inner workings,
and created,
and wrote stories
for the ones yet to come,
and cleaned the dust
from your own corners within.

I see your eyes.
And I know they hold tales
that can never be told.

Wow, sister...

You have really let yourself go.

And you have gone so far
that your eyes take me on a journey...

So I, too, can let myself go.

Thank you, dear sister.

For letting yourself go...

There...

To all the places wild, raw, and true.

So I can know the path is safe.

So I can feel the prayers
you laid down on the path
as it twists and turns.

So when I get lost
in the spirals,

I can remember

that this
is how
to find my way

to letting myself go.

Home.

Enter the Temple, Sister

Enter into the Temple, Sister,

We have draped it in lush red tapestries, blankets, cushions, and lavish altars... just. for. YOU.

Allow us to wash your feet with water fresh from the land,
sprinkled with rose petal prayers.

Fall into our arms as we run our fingers through your hair,
tell us stories that have sat untold in the caverns of your heart.

Braid your sister's hair as she tells you what she is dreaming up,
as you get the honor of glimpsing into her most treasured visions.

Sit at the feet of the elder as she teaches you to spin your knitting needles, weaving dreams into creation, and pulling at the threads of humble wisdom unspooling from her lips.

Breathe with us and howl the sounds of ancient rememberings...
See yourself as wisdom keeper, and feel her return to your bones.

Hear the songs of those who hold the keys with codes in word and melody... To call us back into our bodies and center.

Be here with us, sister. Simply to BE.

Sister Magic

We remember ourselves more deeply
with the reflections of one another.

Through your pain expressions,
I understand mine more deeply.

Through witnessing your beauty,
I know myself more as that beauty.

Through your reclamation of power,
I am re-energized in my own.

Through your wisdom sharing,
mine flows more freely.

Through your truth
I am more liberated.

Through witnessing you,
and being witnessed by you,
I witness myself.

Through being heard by you,
I feel my voice express more confidently.

Through dancing around the fire alongside you,
my body releases lifetimes worth of bound up energy.

The gifts of the connection of shared sacred space,
with you, are immeasurable.

My dear Sister

You are my sister because we are born of the same Earth.

You are my sister because we were raised under the same umbrella of collective wounding and conditioning.

You are my sister because we share stories of 'not enough', 'too much', 'me too' - and - 'reclamation', 'remembering', 'being'.

You are my sister because I want to see you Whole, Healed, Healing, Balanced, and living as Love.

You are my sister because I want the best for you.
In all ways. All-ways.

You are my sister because I celebrate you...
Your wins, your yesses, your no's.

You are my sister because when you stand in your own truth, you speak truth that ignites rememberings of my own.

You are my sister because women need to share our stories in safe spaces... To be heard, to clear them, to rewrite them, to remember them... and I want to hear yours.

You are my sister because I honor all women.

You are my sister.
For these reasons and thousands more.

I don't need our relations to be blood or bone or familial or even of a soul connection to want to celebrate you.

I don't need our connection to be personal to care about your empowerment and your healing and your wholeness.

I don't need to even know you to be cheering you on, praying for you, wishing you the best.

I don't need to have your love for me in return to want to hold a space for you of non-competition, non-judgement, and unconditional positive regard.

So yes, you're my sister.

I will throw that term around in ways that may look like I am doing so lightly, flippantly, carelessly, meaninglessly...

but I assure you, I have thought this through.

I will sprinkle Sisterhood in the pockets that you will forget about, only for you to reach in months later and find a surprise glimmer of hope and connection.

I will toss it,
spread it,
and speak it a thousand times over...

Until ALL OF MY SISTERS REmember that
WE are not
in any of this
alone.

Sister may sound like a *pretty, simple,* and *loving* term.

But when I say it...

I include unconditional love for the totality and wholeness of you.

The rage, the tears, the bitch, the witch, the hurts, the forgotten layers, the yet-to-be-uncovered bits, the muffled, the uncertain, the grief, the sad...

And the brilliance, the magic, the radiance, the beauty, the truth underneath the truth, the love, the shine, the potency, the Goddess, the One.

Sure... I may also question myself whether others *mean it* when they say it...
And then...
I will REmember over and over again...

That I mean it.

In the deepest of the deep.
The darkest of the shadow.
The most rooted of the roots.

I trust it.
I will soften in to it.
I will dive in to it.

Because it doesn't matter if anyone else means it.
I do.
And it matters to me.

I also vow to REmember that it is not for me to judge or to project anything at all into another woman's Sisterhood.

Not today.
Not any day.
You do you, sister.

In your own way.

.

With more love than I can express,

I honor YOU, Sister.

XO XO - Jessica

Mythological Divine Feminine

I don't worship a mythological Divine Feminine figure
in the sky, or one locked within the mysteries of the Earth.

I simply breathe and watch women wander through forests,
picking up leaves of soul fragments and integrating them.

I don't worship Divine Feminine idols or ideals
from a far off land or time beyond time.

My religion is heart-outpourings of truth that nutrify the mind,
where women come to be who they be.

I don't worship at an altar made up of God-figures
turned woman-figured-God.

The sacrament here is sister-laughter-turned-remembering,
at the temple of the body - where mine meets yours in dance.

I don't worship an unattainable idea of Divine Femininity
one 'must' become or achieve to embody.

I gather the women for us all to connect the holy dots
of knowing we are already all we seek to be.

The Mysteries

The ancient Goddess mysteries
are not a mystery.
They were not lost in history.
They are living
through the remembering
of Herstory... Your-story.
Your story of Rising,
Reclaiming, Rebirthing,
Returning to the wisdom
within your very own body.

Shedding the slithering layers
of the ways they said were 'right'.
And instead going left.
Leaving it all behind
to forge a path
that has remembered itself
through salten tears
and dancing our way
to ecstatic freedom.

Let us initiate ourselves.
Over and over again.
Initiating liberation
within and without.
Igniting the flame
within the lantern we carry,
lighting the path for ourselves
and those who say yes to walk it.

Empty Vessel

Fill me up
let me overflow

pouring out
all things holy.

Empty me out
again and again

ready to receive
without end.

Chalice

You are the Sacred Chalice of the Ancient Mysteries.
Your body holds the key to unlock all you need to know.
You hold all that has ever been remembered and forgotten.
You are made of the finest Gold and Jewels of the Earth.
You are one with and as The Eternal Divine Feminine.
You are a vessel of endless, eternal Divine Flow.
You sustain life with Infinite Abundance.
You hold miraculous Healing Power.
You are a Wisdom Keeper.
You are the Holy Grail.
You are a living
Temple.
You
are
the
one
and
only.
YOU,
Beloved,
are a walking
expression of all that is Holy.
You are the Sacred Chalice of the Ancient Mysteries.

She Flows

The Priestess flows within your Blood.
The Ones before, and
You, before,
have laid down offerings for this moment to arise
when YOU
would Remember, once more
the YOU
you have always been...
Priestess.

The Priestess IS your Blood
the blood that connects us all
the blood that flowed from the bodies
of the mothers' mothers' mothers'
the grandmothers' grandmothers' grandmothers'
the Priestesses.
Every... One... of them...
of US...
of YOU.

We are here
Remembered
Reclaimed
Rebirthed
Re-Initiated
Priestess, YOU are here.

This Priestess Bloodline connects us all
Everything is within this Blood...
the ancient encoding of our own prayers
the cellular memory of infinite lifetimes
the frequency of the Earth and Stars
vibrations of Wisdom,
the Wisdom of the Wild Ones
the Remembered Ones
the Priestesses.

The Priestess flows within your Blood.
The Priestess IS your Blood.
This Priestess Bloodline connects us all.
Priestess, YOU are here.
It is Remembered. It is Initiated. It is NOW.

To my Priestess Sisters and Initiates

Living Temple

May I be a living Temple of Love.

Blessings and Crystals on the Altar.

Compass Rose windows and Rose Honey Sacrament.

Holy Waters as Communion flowing from the Chalice.

The Embodiment of Wholeness and Prayer.

Flames lit on beeswax candles. Doors and arms open.

Draped in Red velvet and White lace.

Wearing Trust like a starry crown.

Filled with gilded mirrors that gaze back.

Built from the Earth's bones, with a foundation to last lifetimes.

Moss and ivy becoming one with hallowed stone.

Pinnacles piercing clouds, aiming towards the heavens.

Domes, arches, and breathtaking ornate beauty.

A Circular Cathedral in the Center of a bustling Italian square.

An artifact of glorious architecture that stirs life within passers by.

Visited in reverence by those of the same heart.

Surrounded by Sisters of Mercy.

An ancient relic of well-preserved mysteries, unveiled for all to see.

A Sanctuary that holds the imprint of the Divine.

A Chapel with Our Lady at the threshold.

A shrine of Truth. A church of all things ordinary.

Imparting Luminous Revelation within all who look inside.

Resounding echoes of stillness and silence, laughter and song.

Where all is spoken and held... Prayers, Griefs, Hopes, Dreams.

Where ritual, invocations, and chants are venerated and shared.

Where sermons are spoken in honor of the Goddess.

Where written symbols and words are deciphered.

A Sacred Space with endless interpretations.

A house of Anointment and Consecration.

Gratitude outpouring like a Wellspring.

Offering Abundant Love as Charity.

Breathing Eternal Devotion.

Planting seeds as tithe.

Ever in service.

A Holy Place.

I Am.

Priestess

The Priestess lays prayers
at the altar of her inner temple
creating and curating
sanctuaries of resilience
to hold for herself and others.

The Priestess holds vigil
for all that has been lost
or changed shape.
For all that has transitioned
is fertile fodder for what's to come.

The Priestess tends the wild
within and without,
knowing herself as wind and wildfire,
to embody the medicine
and wisdom of wholeness.

The Priestess knows ecstatic bliss,
the penetrative persuasion of passion,
sensory pleasure, and joy,
the feel of each petal and thorn
with every morsel of her being.

The Priestess knows heartache.
The holiest holes of the deepest aches.
She feels them as the infinite well,
so she can taste the nectar
of both allness and no-thing-ness.

The Priestess has traveled
through lifetimes and timelines
within the innermost corners of her heart,
to know shadow and light
not as duality, but as oneness.

The Priestess remembers herself
as a mirror, reflecting truth,
as a sister, nurturing women,
as a ceremonialist in everyday life,
and as keeper of the mysteries.

The Priestess is simply human.
Walking her walk, messy and mundane.
Each step in devotion to exploration
and deepening into the sweet humble path
of a life well lived.

The world is your altar
And you are the stone

Place yourself with intention
And let your heart be your home

Priestess duties

Priestessing is
hand washing mascara
from tear filled revelations
soaked into eye pillows
marked as living proof
of unraveling oneself from
tapestries of ancestral traumas.

Priestessing is
warming the kettle
to remove wax from sheep's fur
poured out in overflow
in Divine reminders that
SHE cannot be contained
and messiness is part of the path.

Priestessing is
carefully picking up the pieces
of shattered glass shards
that once held prayers
now popped open
and released by fire's flames
burning away the old.

Priestessing is
saying no
as a complete sentence
with fierce love and compassion
and simultaneous devotion to truth
knowing that no is a permission granter
for deepening yesses.

Song of Motherhood

The song of motherhood
that only gets sung in secret
has lyrics of longings
for a life unavailable to be lived.

The rhythms become
that of the day to day,
and the wild tune of once-freedom
fades slowly in the background.

In the shower, she sings
the melody of daydream swirlings
and lucid visions
of unbound becoming.

Cycles come, and
the longing to howl
with the full moon wildlings
pulls at her skin.

Then, she looks over
at the face of her beloved child,
and remembers her contentment,
at least for now...

To my inner little girl

Your world will soon shatter.
You won't even realize it.
You'll simply sink into a hole.
You'll stay there for a while.

You'll learn sadness and betrayal.
Your heart will break open.
You will feel wildly broken.
Stay soft through it all, dear one.

You will make it through.

You will lose yourself a little.
But what you find on the other side...
Will be more brilliant than you know.

Don't fight yourself.
Don't add shame to your heart.

Just hold onto hope and love.
You'll find your way back to yourself.
And you'll be more you than you know.
I love you. You've got this.

Pink

I open myself back up to the color pink.

Pink as:

Playfulness and Optimism
Innocence and Compassion
Nurturance and Love
Kindness and Approachability

Passion and Femininity
Inner Peace and Calm
Noticing and Affection
Kinship and Friendship

Perhaps I first shut her out of my life
When they told me to grow up

Perhaps I disliked her
When they said I was childish

Perhaps I separated myself from her
When the world no longer felt safe in pink

Perhaps I cut myself off from her
When they told me to be like a man

Perhaps I distanced myself from her
When other women felt like my enemy

Perhaps I rejected her
When I rejected what they called femininity

Perhaps I shunned her
When I shunned myself

Perhaps
I
Now
Know a deeper way

Perhaps
I
Now remember and
Know myself

Perhaps
I have reclaimed
Nine year old me and all
Kid layers of myself

Perhaps
It is time to own, that
Never did I cut her out fully, she has always been my
Kindred heart

Perhaps
I remember
Nothing about myself was unworthy
Keen awareness brought me back home

Perhaps
I shall allow myself to once again
Notice the world through Rose colored glasses and
Kismet Trust

My sweet holy child.

A most sanctified reflection.

Of the heart's deepest hidden corners.

To my teenager

A subtle shame
casts its gaze over our hearts
in teenage years
when we finally begin
to see the world
through growing eyes.

The shame of wishing
to be wild, free, untamed,
uncensored, unconstrained,
when all we see is a vision of
"adulthood" through
the carefully crafted living example
of parents, teachers, and those
"responsible" for us.

We see the world in its limits,
pushing us into boxes
to fit into the systems,
and a fire is lit within
perhaps for the first time in this way...
the fire to be the full self.

Just then, we may begin to feel
"different", un-belonged,
unconforming,
hormones raging and coursing...
Longing for independence
while living in a structure
where that very thing is only an illusion.

Some of us reach that place
and pause or retract,
or travel down the road
that has been carved
by the ones before.

And sometimes,
the inner fire
gets a breath of life
and we stir ourselves
into our own wild.

Knowing we aren't
"different" than 'them'...
rather, we are differentiating
ourselves,
freeing ourselves,
carving a path of truth
that is made for only us,
a path that grows us
into being.

My child,
please,
fly into the wild unknown...
create a path
where your feet love to dance,
where your voice
loves to shout and howl,
where you feel most
YOU...
ALL of YOU.

I will stay in my "role",
ever caring, and
"responsible,"
only because I am
'able to respond'
and it has been my promise
to show you comfort
so you can eventually
feel comfortable enough
to grow your own way.

But I wish,
for you
to be you.
Not an image
of responsibility
you think you see
in me
or anyone else.

Fall far from this tree,
sweet wise Crow...
strengthen your wings,
learn to fly,
fall some more,
stumble and play,
explore,
find your inner wild,
go as far as you can...
and remember,
you are not intended to be
anyone but you.

Listen.

Listen.

Listen.

Keep Listening.

Listen some more.

Listen again.

Listen.

Listen.

Listen.

Secrets

Dearest Woman,

I know you have secrets.
Secret art which has yet to be seen by anyone but you.
Written words that stir magic, but sit in the secret cave of your heart.
Journals, notes, and musings filled with secret medicine.
Secret wisdom, that maybe doesn't quite feel like wisdom.

You keep them secret, and just for you.
Perhaps because they are intended to be that way.
Perhaps because you don't feel they are worthy to be shared.
Perhaps because sharing our secrets is opening us up vulnerably.
This is your invitation. To share them. Please.

The world needs your secrets.

So we can remember that our secrets don't need to be kept secret.
So we can remember the secret ways of women.
So we can know that others secretly long for the same thing we do.
So we can remember that wisdom can be simple, complex, polished, unpolished, messy, sacred, Divine, and whole...

And it is worthy of no longer being kept secret.

Just share it! Share it! Share it!

It is time.

Thank you, Beloved

Thank you, Beloved,
for holding the imprint
of remembering
precisely in the moment
when I need it the most.

Thank you, Beloved,
for holding steady ground
while I ebb and flow
and let myself go
into the wild of the wind.

Thank you, Beloved,
for holding the reminder
of staying true
in all of truth's forms
even when unpretty.

Thank you, Beloved,
for the sweetest love
like nectar on my tongue,
for the holy juice
f your soul's embrace.

Thank you, Beloved
for coming back here with me
again and again,
to the freedom
of love's heart center.

Divine Creativity

Dearest Child,

Play! Laugh! Pretend! Create!

Float like the wind, and
paint to reveal wisdom innate.

Sing!
Dance!
Frolic!

And decipher stories symbolic.

For you, dear one, are here to be free.
Not bound by self-limiting energy.

Become yourself
by letting yourself BE.

And pour yourself forth

with DIVINE CREATIVITY

The Holy Harpist

She sits.
Plucking holy threads
of heavenly sound
from thin air.

Weaving them together,
notes of beauty dancing in harmony.

She sits.
On a seat of Grace,
with gentle presence.
Humble in her creation.

Lulling the souls
of the passers by and the ones who wait.

She sits.
Perhaps knowing or unknowing
of the depths
to which her songs reach.

Strumming the chords
of the heart for those with ears to hear.

She sits.
Creating rippling waves
of healing reverberation.
Soothing and otherworldly.

In a sea of mundanity, unmoved by the external.
Steady in her offering.

She sits.
Touching magic and lineage,
one string at a time.
A symphony of Spirit.

Timeless ways of old
resounding and enchanting through her hands.

She sits.
Wielding powerful
acoustic echoes.
Reflecting Ease.

Melodic musings meet the mind.
And the rhythm speaks eternal.

She sits.
Reminding that
the Sacred is everywhere,
whispering its music.

If only we pause,
just for a moment,
to truly listen.

Imperfections

are the symbols

and nuggets

to find our way

home to ourselves

Live Weird

when you live
as your true self

in a way that goes
against the grain

you create ripples of respite
for others just like you

who have felt alone
so they now know it is safe

to live in their unique truth
and to know there are others

who need those same reminders
only they can reflect

don't hold back your weird
it is the ultimate permission slip

and we need everyone
at the helm

The Wild World

Gently

Hands gently open,
holding what flows
loosely, lightly, lovingly.

Hands gently open,
not grasping, attaching,
or holding on.

Hands gently open,
ready to receive
what may come.

Hands gently open,
ready to release
what may go.

Hands gently open,
to embrace another,
and myself.

Hands gently open,
for hands mirror hearts.
Hearts gently open.

The Holy Temple of the Wild

The Holy Temple of the Wild is pulling me in

Enticing me with visions of shedding skin
Beckoning me with the howl of the wind

Invoking me with the smell of soil
Evoking me with the sssssssserpents coil

Summoning me like a siren's song
Bewitching me with dreams dancing all night long

Seducing me with thoughts of stillness
Tempting me with the rose's brilliance

Hypnotizing me with fire's dancing light
Compelling me with hawk in flight

Alluring me with twinkling stars
Awakening me with ancestral scars

Shall I go or shall I stay
The Holy Temple of the Wild calls

and deeply I long to obey

Full Moon Dreaming

Many moons
I have fallen
into the slipstream
of my subconscious

only to find
Divine visuals
dancing in
my dreamscapes

of times
I can no longer discern
were rememberings
or desires never to be.

Alas, they haunt me
in waking times.

The craving eludes me,
and alludes to be,
the sweetest
of temporary memories.

My Prayer

My prayer is wild
as that of Earthen soil
and mossy moonlit stone

My prayer is untamed and raw
primal as blood, bone, and fur
howled out to be heard through time

My prayer has witnessed skin
layers shed unveiling what is real
mirrored in vulnerability by sisters

My prayer has seen holy rage
and the ferocity of a woman scorned
growling her way to freedom

My prayer has wailed with tears
so deep they meet oceans underground
and re-hydrate aquifers

My prayer has danced
rattling this body into remembering
undulating with ugly truth

My prayer has been sung
songs out of tune to re-attune
and hum me back to the heart

My prayer knows no bounds
and extends beyond a nameless God
into the formless of the eternal

My prayer is one of pleasure
ecstatically yessing myself
disentangled from webs of shame

My prayer is as mundane
as washing dirt from my feet
pulling out embedded chestnut needles

My prayer has been spoken
until no words were left
sitting in silence and darkened mystery

My prayer has stayed awake
from one day to the next
laying out every bit to be kissed by flames

My prayer is holy and whole
deeper than words whispered
across closed hands

My prayer is mine
wildly undefined
and un-confined

My prayer is simple
to love and be loved
and remember I AM

Sacred Seeking

Stone stairs and rambling roots
Wise waters and trees of truth
Animal allies and fungi friends
Wearily wandering to the eternal end
Questions and quandaries on my holy heart
Seeking solutions from fertile forest art
Secrets or symbols, analogies or answers
Wise wings flutter ripples of in-dream dancers
Returning me to reason, everything is enough
Restoring resilience and teaching trust
Butterfly bloodlines and creekside codes
Reminding me rooted-ly, Here I am home

Spell Casting

My prayer contains words
they said were curses
and I say are spelling.

My prayer is oracular
cast with intention
wild and foretelling.

My prayer is heathenous
in cadence with starshine
dancing in moonlit skin.

My prayer is holy and whole
it does no harm and
knows no sin.

Move with Divine Purpose

I move with Divine Purpose
watching invisible rose petals
swirl up at my feet with every step
dispersing their fragrant blessings.

I move with Divine Purpose
swaying these hips in spirals
seducing myself into flow
walking towards desired action.

I move with Divine Purpose
shaking these goddess thighs until prayer
drips out of my mind and through my hair
across the stars and onto the Earth.

I move with Divine Purpose
rattling my bones and drumming my heart
singing prayer through echoed leaves
looking into the mouth of mossy waters.

I move with Divine Purpose
my hands mirroring movements of my soul
tracing scent of Rosemary-stained fingertips
tasting ancestral blessings in salted air.

I move with Divine Purpose
speaking swords of truth
cutting away cords that bind
weaving new ways of relating.

Your Allies Remember

When you notice yourself forgetting who you are,
falling away from your center,
drifting towards the darkened mystery...

Find the sacred item nearest you,
a leaf, fire, flowers, or a freeform stone,
and ask it to remember who you are while you are away...

Place all of your Trust into this ally
that it may hold the knowing
so you can fully let go and flow into the unknown.

No need to hold your identity
or attachments where you are going,
dissolve it all into the infinite expanse and release.

When your silent prayers become pleas...
breathe them into your ally
without needing to know anything at all, simply breathe.

Don't grasp onto remembering,
for it lives just outside your grasp.
Simply speak, sing, sigh, and cry with your sacred guide.

Dance deeply into the forgetting,
so you can also forget who you are not.
And only when you truly forget you have forgotten
will your ally remind you of who you be...

Pink Fragrant Rose

Pink fragrant rose
turns to gold
as it meets the heat
of alchemy.

Like blackened coal
turns into full clarity
of a crystalline diamond
in just the right moment.

Push and pull.
Ebb and flow.
Release and unfurl.
The new becomes you.

Once the essence
is catalyzed,
it can never return
to it's former state.

We can wish the petals back,
the flame turned ember...
But it is time now dear,
step forward and remember.

I See

I see Hawk in shapes of moonlit trees.
I see Owl in patterns of stone.
I see my grandmother as a child
when I look into my bones.

I see stillness
in movement of streams
I see what I look for...
Hope, Magic, and Dreams.

I see lost blood in petal and thorn.
I see longing and ache in thundering storms.
I see myself healed,
whole, and reborn.

I see the Divine Mother
In swirling strands of fallen hair
I see messages from the unseen
Every, every, everywhere.

Wisdom from Hawk

Like the eyes
of the Hawk...

See yourself.

Look within.

Don't forget.

The Hawk doesn't forget
to fly
to hunt
to breathe
to be.

Why do you
forget your nature?

Don't let the weight of the world
make you sink deep into the heaviness of despair.
You will stay there -
at the bottom of the cauldron.
Stuck and scorched.

Instead... meet each morning...

Before you remember
the weight of the world...

When you've still forgotten
your responsibilities
from the glorious night
of Dreaming Divine.

Sit in that forgetting.
To remember YOU.

The YOU underneath it all.

Remember.

Like the Hawk meets the day.

Remember your nature.

Deer Visions

I have died, as the deer,
and rebirthed, as the deer.

She licks the dried black blood
from my once-aching wounds.
Honoring and receiving my death
as nutrition for new life.

I lay dead
at her feet.
And rest in the darkness
of her womb.

She holds me gently
with love.

Knowing all
is in Divine order.

Born of the Elements

Water
Wind
Earth
and
Fire

Born of the elements
I am wild

Water
Wind
Earth
and
Fire

I am the one
Great Mother's child

I am the Earth

I am the one
I am the all
I am the nothing
I am the call

I am the owl
I am the hawk
I am every step
Of my sacred walk

I am the winter
I am the autumn
I am the summer
Springing forward

I am the earth
I am the clouds
I am the squirrel
Squirreling around

I am the beaver
I am the dam
I am the wool
On the little lamb

I am the fox
I am the hound
I am the echoes
On this ancient ground

I am the sea
I am the salt
I am the source/rer
Of all things water

I am the weaver
I am the web
I am all things flow
And all things ebb

I am the child
I am the mother
I am my life's creator
And it's lover

I am so empty
I am so full
I am listening
When I hear the soul's pull

Air

I wish to learn of the Air as it dances
like leaves in a breeze.

The Air in its stillness,
the pause in between.

I wish to learn of the Air as it teases
through my hair like a comb.

The Air as it moves,
carving mountains and stone.

I wish to learn of the Air as it feeds
the sacred fires flames.

The Air as it plays,
moving waters like a game.

I wish to learn of the Air as it carries
the winged ones in flight.

The Air as it breathes
the holy breath of life.

Mighty winds on mighty wings...
Teach me, teach me, teach me these things.

Appalachian Embrace

Never have I felt as home as I do
the way these mountains
wrap their limbs
around my bones

Feet held by
the warm damp soil
of decayed pieces
and parts of the whole

Shaded by the ones
standing tall in all directions
Encircled by allies
on foot and in flight

I am here, now
Called to myself
by this wind and sky
vibrating the imprint of ME

Earthen Home

Dragonfly
Firefly
Butterfly
Eye to sky

Spider
Lavender
Hellbender
Remember

Queen Bee
Hickory
Rosemary
Set me free

Oak tall
Stream song
Deer strong
Fear gone

Squirrel
Turtle
Turkey
Friend I see

Hummingbird
Squishy worm
Roots in Earth
Prayer in word

Snake skin
Unnamed kin
Body I'm in
Shed again

Turkey tail
Chanterelle
Bath from the well
Weave this spell

Community
Only trees
This I see
My HOME, the key...

I am Learning

I am learning
The browsing patterns of the white-tailed herd
of deer kin through the land.
Light-half afternoons through the trail.
Dark-half mornings up the hillside.
Six sisters. Together.

I am learning
The places where the sky meets the sun.
Dancing through the seasons.
Pink sunrises and mountain mist.
Star speckled darkness. Clarity and cloudiness.
Hawk shaped tree-shadow at winter's midnight.

I am learning
The quickening of compost.
Fallen leaves nutrifying the earthen path.
Becoming one with all that is and is not.
Consumed and excreted by the tiny crawlers
and crawling mycelium.

I am learning
How my cycles mirror this
deepening at-one-ment divested from man-made systems.
Returning to the holy of the wild.
Deer sister co-regulating my system.
Hawk brother reminding me to fly.
Mycelium grandparents remembering me back home.

Emotions are an Ocean

Emotions are an ocean
A vast visionary field
Dive in and wail
Swim with fins spread wide

See what you can sea
Only what is revealed
With eyes fully adjusted
To complete darkened depths

Mermaid Musings

Waves swell alongside the rhythm of my heart
Cresting and crashing through my illusions
Drifting through the currents of my mind
Letting myself be fully taken by the tides
Surrendering into the womb-home of the Earth

The return to self happened in an instant
A single breath of salted sea air
Merged my body and soul into reunion
Wholeness embraced me tightly from within
Lingers of melancholy wrung themselves out

The waves sung me a song of homecoming
Summoning me back to my own bones
Each thrash an invocation of remembering
Each ebb and flow teaching how far I've strayed
From the simple truth of my own knowing

Called now to continue forth in action
Walking the path I know to be true
Each step towards myself and my devotions
Not through the easy, well-trodden rut I've carved
The only way through is leaping into a new current

Ocean Eyes

Why oh why
does the ocean insist
on flowing through my eyes
again and again...

Why are they such lovers,
drawn to one another
as the moon
draws the tides...

I wish to be of the mountains,
steady and rooted,
anchored in stone,
silent and still...

And yet, I am one with the sea,
crashing and thrashing,
infinite unexplored depths,
cyclical in flow...

Darkness and salt,
anointed by my own waters,
waves pouring endlessly,
I am learning to swim...

My prayer is no longer
for the ocean to calm her waves,

desiring to change the nature of the sea
in order to satisfy my comfort...

I celebrate her bigness now.

I simply ask to learn
to swim her currents with grace.

Feathers

Feathers
Fluttering into
Fire's
Flames during
Fall's
Frigid night

Familiars
Forever
Facilitating
Favors

Fae
Folk
Fervently
Foretell of

Fierce
Fractals
Fanning the
Faith

Feelings
Foresee
Feasible
Forgiveness

Fertility
Flows as
Fresh
Fodder

Fare thee Well...

Full Moon Musings

When the moon is full
my soul is stirred awake
with a wild ancient song

I lay in sleepless surrender
her essence piercing through my window
and the windows of my heart

She shines her elder reflection
painting stories in starlight
casting shadows and spells

Her muses dancing through my mind
with reckless abandon
evoking what normally lies hidden

My heart begins to name its longings
and all of them are to return
to deepened layers of myself

Like Luna returns to her fullness
each cycle steady in ebb and flow
shadow and light in whole glory

How can I sleep in a time like this
when the silver face of the goddess
brings herself all the way to me
to remember me back home...

Imbolc

Seeds stir under snow-sparkled soil.

In the liminal mystery
between half-formed dreams
and boundless becoming.

We see the sacred flame's first spark,
and feel the warmth of the Earth-womb
readying herself for our emergence.

It is time to be birthed...
and return again.

In sweet time
buds blossom
petals unfurl

slowly
then all at once

touching nearby thorns

fragrant

The Calling of Spring

It is time.

Time to wake up and walk forward.
Time to blossom and emerge.
Time to open and stretch.
Time to expand.

Wipe the sleep from your eyes.
The day is calling.
Your path is calling.

This time, when you wake,
wake anew.

Follow the call
of your true nature.
It knows the way.
It knows the pattern
of your divine unfurling.

Spiritual
Untangling
Meets
Mysterious
Existential
Re-examining

Sensations of Earth

I lay my body upon the body of the Earth
Soft moss cushions my resting cheek
My heartbeat echoes with the pressing of my ear on stone

The smell of the soil captivates me
I close my eyes and breathe it in
The intense scent of life invokes my presence

I crawl over to the oak roots
As they beckon me with their winding wisdom
Watching entire worlds birthed in microcosms

I look up to the rising moon
The standing tall ones encircle me
Their branches seemingly as high as the stars

I hear the hoot of the owl
Leaves crackling under footsteps
And the katydids calling in the night

The stream trickles onward
Singing me back into myself
Songs of release and re-presencing

I drink from the spring
Tasting clarity and aliveness
And earthen minerals on my tongue

I feel the warmth of summer's night
Wrapping me with arms of love
My body exhales and softens

Dried mud lingers between my toes
The wild waters have evaporated from my hair
My cells re-vibrating and reverberating

For a brief-yet-infinite moment in time
I allow myself into the forest within
She has waited, and welcomed me home

It only took an afternoon wander
To find my way back
All the way to me

Thank you, momma Earth
For holding me so tenderly
And holding remembering when I forget

All-night Fire

Watching flames dance
through the saltwater gaze
of tear-filled eyes.

Holding vigil
from sun-down to
morning's sliver moonrise
and dawn's gentle light.

Naming hundreds of prayers
for before, for release, for ease
for now, for remembering, for wholeness
ror what has yet to be walked - in beauty.

Clearing lines and lineages
with a sacred forgiveness
and compassion.

Countless herbs, flowers, and seeds
collected over the moons before,
now offered as sacrament.

Laying an offering,
of holy earthen death,
for healing through body and lines.

Speaking stories
of close beloveds departed,
ritual and prayer in their name.
Release and honoring.

Leaves falling into flames
from the tall ones above,
as acknowledgements of blessing
in their artistic peak.

In this holy bone-fire,
on all Hallows' eve,
under clear starry skies.

Until embers and ash
collect in the cauldron
of remembrance.

Nestled in the mountain's embrace,
crackles of wood creating
fire song on one side,
rushing creek on the other.

Prayers for realness,
and dismantling,
acknowledgements of learning,
privilege and right-relationship.

Let whispers of these prayers
reach your ears
from across the lands...
for YOUR name was spoken in blessing.

Imprinted.
Re-imprinted.
Integrated.
Re-integrated.

Autumn Queen

She wears a crown of Laurel
Oak roots hold up her silvering hair
Glittering mud under her fingernails
Cheeks blushed by chilled fall air

She is the Autumn Queen
Guided by Hawk and Owl
You see her in red Maple leaves and
Hear faint echoes of her primal howl

She tends the vigil fire
All through the night
As you lay your blessings one by one
Neath the full moon's light

She feeds you soup and squash
Warm drinks of spiced cider
You feel the call of attunement
As she invites you to dream wilder

She whispers to you through the unseen
To slow down, rest, and retreat
While you seek comfort and respite
She kisses your cheek as you sleep

Tired Eyes

My eyes are tired.
Tired of looking at images,
scrolling interwebs instead of innerwebs,
reading words on pages.

My eyes are tired.
Tired of seeing the aches of the world,
noticing needs going unmet,
and places where love hasn't fully reached the core.

My eyes are tired.
Tired of taking it all in,
watching and witnessing,
perceiving and creating meaning.

My eyes are tired.
So tired that I deeply long to solely observe moss,
and catch glimpses of morning dew
sparkling in the sun's rays.

My eyes wish to rest.
Under the clouds,
eyelids closed and heart open,
beholding only sounds.

Where the only visions are internal,
prophesying the eternal,
or the simplicity of
nothing at all.

May my eyes stay open,
to see sights of stillness,
recognizing what needs recognizing,
and allowing the rest to rest.

Winter Blessings

Blessings of the deepest darkening.

Blessings of rich fertile aliveness within the emptiness.

Blessings of stillness and silence.

Blessings of deepened dreaming and divination.

Blessings of the dark moon on this longest night.

Blessings of cave like wonders.

Blessings of ancient whispers.

Blessings of the bones of trees.

Blessings of light and illumination.

Blessings of holy wholeness.

Blessings of sweet simple ceremonial moments.

Blessings of evergreen rememberings.

Blessings of slowing down to breathe it all in.

Blessings of warmth to the places that need it most.

Blessings of the owl mother wrapping it all in her wings.

Blessings of ease when cultural norms ask so much

during a time of the deep soul call to experience so little.

Evergreen

This year, I am wintering as an Evergreen

I shall not lose my leaves, or go into dormancy
I will thrive amongst the sleeping ones

Plenty of summers, I was in my winter's cave
living within my own cycle and spiral

I spent many moons resting
and no longer feel a need to let go

While my kin are in hibernation
I shall tend my own roots

Not needing to mirror what they are doing
or consider what they are doing

I long to know winter from this place
of full aliveness - even with reason to turn inward

And I shall live it thrivingly...
Verdant, and consistently creating

Standing tall in cold, dark, difficult times
Wintering as an Evergreen

Beauty in Winter's Death

Beauty in the dying
Beauty in the letting go
Beauty in the dormancy
Beauty in the inner resourcing
Beauty in the thriving underneath what looks like death
Beauty in the shedding unnecessary bits
Beauty in the trust that vibrancy will return
Beauty in the cycles and seasons of life
Beauty in the life underneath the seen
Beauty in what thrives in between
Beauty in the unclear skies
Beauty in the stillness
Beauty in the falling
Beauty in the wild way
Beauty in the uncommon
Beauty under the surface
Beauty beholding itself
Beauty in humility
Beauty in the mists
Beauty in the mystery
Beauty in the beauty

Just when winter's cold,
hardened darkness
begins to feel
on the brink of unbearable...

A tiny green shoot
springs up
from decaying leaves
bringing hope
that blossoms
are soon to come.

Pink Skies

I wish I could share with you this sky.
Her bright pale-pink clouds,
periwinkle and rolling lavender hues.

Reducing it to words,
or seeing through camera's lens,
box the infinite into something small.

I try to share it,
yet the moment I do,
I am pulled out of that mystical world.

But here, me and the sky,
we are in another place together.
One of magic and prayer.

She comforts me behind winter's branches.
Bringing hope just when I feel blue,
right when I need a holy embrace.

I breathe in this majesty,
these colors more than color,
these alive energies calling me back to myself.

In the deepened darkening of winter,
the sun comes with reminders
that each day has a little light.

Just before it sets beyond the mountain,
it kisses the sky once more,
singing its songs of 'all is well'.

Full Circle

The pleas and prayers
I spoke into the winds
years ago, moons ago, days ago
float back to me
on the breath of the Divine

returning to my ears
encircling my heart
sacred reminders calling me forth
into action

each letter and word
heard clearly

each one a spell
casted upon myself
here and now
from some wisened place
within

Lineage Love

You
are
the
living,
walking,
breathing
embodiment
of
all
the
hopes,
prayers,
and
dreams
of
your
ancestresses.

Live
as
such.

Holy Heathen

My Momma
Witchy and Wild
Loving and Free
Teaching me
to be
The Holy Heathen
within

Teach me to love my shadow
as much as my light
for neither is too bright

Teach me hope
in spite
of fear and uncertainty
when I know certainly
you will be there

Thank you to my momma
for teaching me how to BE
not HOW to be

Thank you, momma,
and may it be
today that you once again see

I love you.

Written by my daughter, Crow, as a birthday gift to me, April 4, 2023

Day Dance

Dawn awaits the
hope filled moments
before the rise of the sun.

Sun carrying light to the day
fueling warmth, growth, and fun.

Noon around the corner, sending
morning to break away.

Calming dimness calls for dusk
to beckon the radiant moon.

Rest now, my sweet darling
magical dreams await you.

Written by my mother, Cristine M. Lestage, June 3, 2023

Waiting

I hate to see the day go,
The warmth and brightness gone.
The night is like a shadow,
Waiting, waiting for the dawn.

And then, and then the dawn,
The shiny brilliance comes,
Moonbeams depart,
The foggy darkness gone.

With the darkness goes my sorrow:
All my tears are taken too.
The newborn dawn brings the morrow
And I sing when the skies are blue.

Written by my grandmother, Charlene Bertha Bahls, Autumn 1958

Sister Blessing

If the life's storms rage
If danger surrounds you
Send your eyes upwards
To the father, who loves you.

.

Originally written in German:

Wenn des Lebens Stürme toben
Wenn Gefahr disch rings umgibt
Richte deinen Blick nach oben
Zu dem Vater, der dich liebt.

Written by my great great grandmother, Charlotte Marie Margarethe Petzhold Kulosa, to her sister Dora, Dresden Germany, March 19, 1906

Sweet Soul...
the answer to our prayers...

that one day,
the ones yet to come,
the ones yet to walk,
would remember.

that the ones down the line
would re-weave the threads.

You are here.
You are here now.

We are with you.
We never left.
We were always
right here.

In your blood and bones.

Humming the heartbeat tune
to sing you back
into remembering.

Thank you.

- Your Ancestresses

Dearest Grandmothers...

Oh, Thank You!

Thank you for holding the
simplicity
when I strayed.

And for holding the space
when I strayed.

Thank You.
Thank You.
Thank You.

- I Remember

Thank you.

Thank you.

Thank you.

Author's Note

In recent years, I have been deepening into the embodied understanding of the concept 'doing what we were drawn to as a child in order to find what is most true to our souls'. Writing the words within this book unveiled a deeper sense of that for me.

I remember always cherishing journals as a kid. I would beautifully decorate them, vision-board-style on the outside, and fill them with words that felt like medicine to me. In high school, a friend and I decided we would write a "new kind of bible" for the religion of LOVE. It was a 'silly' passing thought at the time, but one I felt deep in my bones. In sifting through some old writings and journals during the writing of this book, I found a journal of quotes and poems I curated in 2003 with musings about Love and the heart, written book-style with a title and sections. Exactly 20 years ago. Love is still a lifelong anchor for me. Lastly, I found another quotes & poems book I curated in 2016, cover to cover, as a way to heal from a challenging life-transition and orient myself to a deepened sense of who I AM as a Sacred being. This book mirrors that, as I am in a mirrored-timeline on the other side of a similar transition.

Turns out, poetic and symbolic words have been medicine for me long before I truly knew that this was a lifelong theme of mine.

We know before we know.
We know who we are before we know who we are...
We simply reveal layers of ourselves, as we walk our paths,
that show us we are who we have always been all along...
we are simply Remembering ourselves more deeply.

Acknowledgements

To all the women I have ever met, Thank you!
Each one of you I crossed paths with, taught me about myself.

To all the women I have ever loved, Thank you!
Each one of you I have embraced and been embraced by, has been the deepest love and medicine I could have imagined.

To all the women who live out loud, Thank you!
Each one of you has inspired my own impassioned expressions.

To all the women who live silently, or with gentle voice, Thank you!
Each one of you reminds me of my desire for stillness and humility.

To all the women who hold women's circles, Thank you!
You carried the imprint so I could find my way into my own.

To all the women who have yet to be held by a circle, Thank you!
You give me reason to hold the Devotion of my work in the world.

To all the women who have written & published books, Thank you!
Each one of you I witnessed, created a deepened Trust that the path forward was walkable.

To all the women who speak in poetic, symbolic ways, Thank you!
Each one of you has helped me find my way home, and taught me a language that spoke so directly to my soul.

Thank you. Thank you. Thank you. I LOVE YOU!

About the Author

Jessica Ricchetti is a Priestess, Mystic, Energy Alchemist, and Author, living in North Carolina, US. She is an enchanting visionary whose heart and soul have traversed many dimensions over infinite lifetimes; her multifaceted brilliance is compelling and palpable from the moment she steps into a room. She is revered as an adept ceremonialist and masterful space holder by many in her community. Her presence is a harmonic coalescence of piercing masculine and feminine acquiescence. True artistry.

Jessica is a devoted mentor and a co-creatress of the efflorescent priestess lineage known as The Alchemical Rose. In addition to authoring two oracle decks, Wisdom of the Shadow and Wisdom of the Feminine, she is the founder of an ever-growing community of sacred sisterhood. She embraces the potent perfection of every moment while playing in realms of ritual each day and lives life itself as ceremony. Jessica serves as a permissionary to all beings, especially women, to trust their magic, embody wholeness, live their truth, and remember the innate wisdom of their infinite self.

Written by my apprentice LUMiN Love-Star, Intuitive Intimacy Priestess

To learn more about Jessica and her work:
www.jessicaricchetti.com

To learn more about Wisdom of the Shadow
and Wisdom of the Divine Feminine:
www.intuitiveartandalchemy.com

May you feel

Love Notes

flowing from the wisdom of your own heart

TO ✦YOUR✦ HEART

May you know that you are worthy of poetry

Poetry written about you
Poetry written by you
Poetry that defies the rules of poetry

Poetry that lives and breathes
Poetry that floats like the breeze
Poetry that arises from looking at leaves
Poetry that inspires you to get up and leave

Poetry that rises up like flames within you
Poetry that burns as passion becomes you

Poetry that writes itself
Poetry that has no words at all
Poetry in motion

Poetry of swirling your hips
Poetry of a gentle kiss
Poetry of sitting in stillness

Poetry that is or isn't prose
Poetry as poetry flows

Write it
Read it
Remember it in your bones

These are the spells
That weave us back home

May you feel a continued deepening into your own

Wholeness

May you feel inspired at witnessing the magic of

Women

May you be ever nourished and held by the

the Wild World

There is ever a longing in my heart
after leaving a sacred space...

More that wishes to be heard,
visions that remain in the unseen...

Human time is far too contained
for the eternal that wishes to flow...

Made in the USA
Middletown, DE
22 December 2023